MW01196053

Inferences At Bridge

W. Dalton

In the interest of creating a more extensive selection of rare historical book reprints, we have chosen to reproduce this title even though it may possibly have occasional imperfections such as missing and blurred pages, missing text, poor pictures, markings, dark backgrounds and other reproduction issues beyond our control. Because this work is culturally important, we have made it available as a part of our commitment to protecting, preserving and promoting the world's literature. Thank you for your understanding.

INFERENCES AT BRIDGE

By W. DALTON
Author of " ' Saturday ' Bridge "

REPRINTED WITH ADDITIONS
FROM "THE SATURDAY REVIEW"

PHILADELPHIA:
J. B. LIPPINCOTT COMPANY
LONDON: THE WEST STRAND
PUBLISHING CO., LD. ● 1909

HARVARD COLLEGE LIBRARY
FROM THE ESTATE OF
MRS. CHARLES ROBERT SANGER
FEBRUARY 19, 1936

PRINTED BY
HAZELL, WATSON AND VINEY, LD.,
LONDON AND AYLESBURY,
ENGLAND.

CONTENTS

CONTENTS

INFERENCES AT BRIDGE

CHAPTER I

GENERAL INFERENCES

It is a well-known fact that a large number of people go through life with their eyes tight shut, or at any rate heavily bandaged. They see and realise the ordinary events which occur within the circle of their own immediate surroundings, under their noses, so to speak, but beyond that they do not pretend to look at all. They never attempt to read between the lines, to put two and two

together, and to draw inferences, correct
or otherwise, from what they see and hear.

Precisely the same principle applies to
the bridge table.   There are many bridge
players—we all know them by the score
—who are quite *au courant* with the
general principles and conventions of the
game, who play their cards intelligently
and well, and who consider themselves,
and are considered, good sound players,
but who never dream of rising to a height
beyond that, or of drawing even the most
simple inferences from what they see
happen during the play of a hand.   To
tell such a one that, in a No Trump game,
when he holds king and two others of
a suit of which the dummy has queen,
knave, ten to five or six, and the dealer
does not touch that suit, the ace of it is
marked to an absolute certainty in his

partner's hand, is to talk to him in a language which he does not understand, yet this is the most simple of all inferences. There are many others of the same kind. They present themselves in almost every hand which is played, but a large majority of people, who play what they are pleased to call intelligent bridge, allow them to pass by utterly unheeded. Such players simply do not notice the obvious inference, or, if some idea of it does flash across their mind, they fail to make a mental note of it at the time for use later in the hand. Herein lies the one and great secret of the success of the first-class player, and thus he sometimes scores so heavily.

It is not by playing any extraordinarily fine coups, or by wriggling cleverly out of difficult positions, that he gains his advantage. It is by drawing inferences at the time, recording them on the tablets of his memory, and acting on the information thus acquired, that he appears at times to possess an almost intuitive knowledge of how the cards are placed. There is really no intuition about it at all. It is simply close reasoning coupled with a careful observation of the fall of the cards.

One day I was sitting behind a friend of mine, watching him play a hand. He is a very keen bridge player, who fancies himself and his own methods more than a little. The score was one game all, and 24 to 8 in his favour. His right-hand adversary dealt and left it to his partner, who declared hearts.

Let us call my friend A. His hand and the dummy's were :

Hearts—Queen, knave, 10, 7, 6, 2
Diamonds—Queen, 7, 4
Clubs—Queen, knave
Spades—Queen, 9

```
┌─────────────────┐
│        B        │
│                 │
│ Y             Z │
│ (dummy) (dealer)│
│                 │
│        A        │
└─────────────────┘
```

Hearts—King, 9, 4
Diamonds—Ace, king
Clubs—King, 9, 6, 5, 2
Spades—Knave, 6, 3

The first five tricks were played as follows :

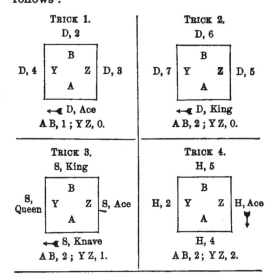

TRICK 1.
D, 2
D, 4   B   D, 3
       Y   Z
       A
←◀ D, Ace
A B, 1 ; Y Z, 0.

TRICK 2.
D, 6
D, 7   B   D, 5
       Y   Z
       A
←◀ D, King
A B, 2 ; Y Z, 0.

TRICK 3.
S, King
S,   B   S, Ace
Queen Y   Z
       A
←◀ S, Knave
A B, 2 ; Y Z, 1.

TRICK 4.
H, 5
H, 2   B   H, Ace
       Y   Z
       A
H, 4
A B, 2 ; Y Z, 2.

TRICK 5.

H, 8

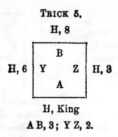

H, King
A B, 3; Y Z, 2.

A then had to lead, and he wanted
two more tricks to save the game. After
considerable thought he led the 6 of
spades, the dealer made the 10 and the
8, discarded a club from Y's hand on
the 8 of spades, and won the game.

I held my peace ; but, after it was
over and all the cards known, A's partner
said to him : " I wonder you did not
put me in with a club so that I could give
you another diamond to make your last
trump.   We should have saved the
game."   A's answer, in a tone of wither-
ing sarcasm, was : " I would have done

so if I had possessed the faculty of seeing through the backs of the cards, but unfortunately I do not possess it. If I had led a club and the dealer had had the ace we should never have made a trick in the suit at all, and I had no possible means of knowing where the ace was. The spade lead was much the best chance of putting you in."

Now, how could the dealer have had that ace of clubs? He had already produced two aces, the ace of ~~diamonds~~ *spades* and the ace of trumps, and was it possible —was it conceivable—that he would have passed the declaration, at that point of the score, with three aces in his hand? Here was an inference which was absolutely sticking out, and which one would have expected to be apparent to the merest tiro at the game, but it was missed,

and missed by a player who invariably
watches the fall of the cards, and who
can generally tell you every card that
has been played. He knew perfectly
well that the dealer had played those
other two aces, but the faculty of putting
two and two together and of deducing
from what he had observed was altogether wanting. The most certain of all
inferences at bridge is that, when the
dealer, after passing the declaration,
produces two aces from his own hand,
he cannot have a third, and that, therefore, the missing ace or aces are marked
to an absolute certainty in one's partner's
hand.

When the dealer has made an original
heart or diamond declaration, the inference that he does not hold three aces is
still there, it is still a sound basis for your

calculations, but it is not quite so reliable. It is possible that he may hold three aces, but that he has thought it a wiser policy to make a strong red suit declaration in preference to going for a somewhat risky No Trump. A glance at your own hand and at the cards exposed in the dummy will generally suffice to clear up this point. If, between you, you have considerable strength in the declared suit, then you may take it for granted that the dealer has not three aces, or he would have declared No Trumps.

When an original red suit declaration has been made, it is always difficult to estimate the strength behind it. There may be a No Trump hand, or there may be just moderate outside assistance, or there may be none; an estimate of this can only be arrived at from future developments, and from the way in which the dealer elects to play his hand. When the dealer passes the declaration, however, there is no such doubt. He is now clearly marked with a hand certainly not much above the average, and probably far below it, and it at once becomes a certainty that he has not three aces. In these advanced days no player would dream of passing the declaration with three aces, however weak the rest of his hand might be, therefore you have this one certainty to begin basing your inferences upon, that when the dealer has passed the declaration to his partner, he cannot possibly hold three aces. Bear this in mind, and make a mental note of it, and remember it the next time your opponent passes. It probably will not be of any assistance to you in that particular case, but at any rate you will have begun to practise the faculty of drawing inferences, and sooner or later that simple inference, that very obvious little inference, will be found to be of great service to you, and to materially assist you in saving a game.

Let us take a very simple instance. The dealer, being 12 up, declares diamonds. Your hand, as third player, and the dummy's are

Hearts—King, 7, 4
Diamonds—Knave, 3, 2
Clubs—9, 6, 4
Spades—Queen, knave, 9, 8

Hearts—Ace, Queen, 10, 6, 2
Diamonds—10, 5, 4
Clubs—8, 7, 2
Spades—10, 3

```
        ┌──────────────┐
        │       B      │
        │              │
        │ Y          Z │
        │ (dummy)      │
        │       A      │
        └──────────────┘
```

Your partner opens with the king of clubs, which the dealer wins with the ace. The dealer then leads ace, king, and queen of trumps, taking all the trumps out, and he then leads the knave of hearts and passes it up. You win with the king, and how are you going to proceed? Your natural impulse is to return your partner's lead of a club, but is this right? Your partner is marked with the king of clubs, but it is by no means a certainty that he has either the knave or 10 as well, and, even if he has, he will then be obliged to open the spade suit. It is an absolute certainty that the dealer has not got the ace of spades, or he would have declared No Trumps, therefore your partner must have it, and the dealer must have the king of spades, as your partner would not have opened the club suit if he held both ace and king of spades. By this method of reasoning

the position of both the ace and king of
spades is clearly marked, and the best,
and the only, chance of saving the game
is to lead the queen of spades, so as to
bottle the dealer's king. If he covers
your queen led, your partner will return
the suit to you, and you will then be able
to return the club suit, so as to utilise
your partner's tenace if he has one.
This is a case where an intelligent player,
who possessed the faculty of drawing
inferences, would be almost certain to
save the game, whereas the unintelligent
and unobservant player would blunder
blindly back with his partner's original
lead, and would lose the game by so
doing, and would then probably remark
that it was unlucky. That word " unlucky " is used to cover a multitude of
blunders at bridge in which luck has no

part—in nine cases out of ten it is not
want of luck but want of observation,
combined with a total lack of the power
of drawing inferences.

CHAPTER II

In the previous chapter great stress was laid on the inference that, when the dealer has passed the declaration, he cannot have three aces in his hand. This is not only the most certain of all inferences at bridge, but it is also one of the most useful in actual practice. When you start primed with the information that the dealer cannot have three aces, and when there is only one to be seen in your own hand or in dummy, it at once becomes a certainty that your partner must have at least one of the remaining three, and very probably more than one. When

15

no ace is visible to you, it becomes an
equal certainty that your partner has at
least two ; and just think how useful the
knowledge that your partner can win
two certain tricks may be to you. You
cannot tell at first which ace or aces he
holds, but you will soon be able to arrive
at that by a process of elimination, and
anyhow you know that he can be de-
pended upon to win two of the tricks
necessary to save the game, so that your
own task is lightened very materially.

This particular form of inference may
be considerably extended, and it can
be applied to other cards besides aces,
although not quite with the same degree
of confidence. When the dealer, having
passed the declaration, produces good
cards in two suits, especially in the two
red ones, it follows that he must be very

weak in the other two, otherwise he would have declared No Trumps.

If he has played from his own hand a winning card in each of three suits, one of such winning cards being an ace, he can at once be marked with nothing of value in the fourth suit, or again he would have declared No Trumps. When he discloses the entire command of one long suit, invariably a black one, it at once becomes obvious that he can have no certain card of entry in any other suit, otherwise he would have gone for what is known as a "one suit" No Trumper.

In this respect—I mean as regards the original declaration of No Trumps—a knowledge of an opponent's idiosyncrasies will sometimes help you to draw correct inferences. When a player who is notorious for making very light No Trump declarations passes the call, you know at once that his hand is very little, if at all, above the average, therefore, if he shows moderate strength in two suits, it is generally safe to assume that he is practically impotent in the other two. On the other hand, when a player who is known to be a sound declarer, possibly even a rather conservative one, declares No Trumps, then you must be prepared for trouble. If you find that he is very weak in one suit, you may take it for granted that he is well ribbed up in the other three, and you should save what you can out of the wreck; but when the declaration has been made by one of those mad No Trump enthusiasts the case is quite different. He may, of course, have a thoroughly sound No

Trump hand, but it is quite as likely that he has nothing approaching a justifiable call, and you should play a much bolder and more offensive game against his declaration than against that of a sound declarer.

An adverse No Trump declaration has a very different effect upon different players. It seems to have a sort of paralysing effect upon some people, especially upon comparative beginners at the game. Directly they hear No Trumps declared against them they appear to lose their heads altogether, and are prepared to give up the game as lost, but this is a very great mistake.

I have never come across any statistics on the subject, but I should think that it is well within the mark to say that not one quarter of the No Trump declarations that are made at the score of love succeed in winning the game on that hand. Many of them lose the odd trick, and some even lose the game. The No Trump declaration is by no means the certain road to success that many players believe it to be, and there is not the slightest occasion to be frightened by it.

It has no terrors for the experienced player—far from it. The first thing that he does, after having satisfied himself that he is not in a position to double with advantage, is to try to realise what the declaration has been made upon. When it has been made by dummy the strength or weakness of it is apparent at once, with the added knowledge that the dealer has not got great strength in either red suit. When the dealer has made the declaration, each opponent has his own thirteen cards, besides those exposed in dummy, to judge from, and also, in the case of the third player, his partner's original opening lead, so that it really is not such an impossible task as it might seem to be.

There are many useful inferences to be drawn. Aces are the first things to think about. If an opponent has not got an ace himself and there is not one in dummy, the declaration has probably been made upon three aces. There may be great strength behind them, or there may not, but in all probability the holding of three aces is the basis of that declaration.

When an original No Trump declaration has been made upon protective strength in all four suits, no inference at all can be drawn from it, but this is only one type of No Trump hand, and not the

most common. The commonest type of
all is on one long suit, usually a black
one, with a varying number of useful
cards in two other suits, and it ought not
to be difficult for the opponents to realise,
early in the hand, what that one long
suit is. Take a very simple instance.
The eldest hand opens with the 2 of
hearts, the dummy puts down only two
clubs, and the third hand has only two.
He, the third player, can at once place
the dealer with at least five clubs, as there
are nine not accounted for and the original
leader, having opened a four-card suit,
cannot hold five clubs, therefore a long
club suit is obviously the foundation of
the No Trump call.

It may not, at first sight, appear to be
very useful to you to know that your
opponent has five cards of a suit in which

you are practically undefended, in fact
that knowledge may be rather terrifying,
but, nevertheless, it gives you great
assistance in dissecting his hand. If he
has great strength, or rather great length,
in one suit, he must be correspondingly
short in another one. His hand only
contains thirteen cards, and when you
can mark him with five cards of one suit,
and possibly three, or even four, of another one, that leaves very few cards
indeed to be divided between the other
two suits, and thus, by the process of
elimination, which is the grand secret of
all counting of hands, you are enabled
to arrive at a correct estimate of which
suit he must necessarily be weak in.
This is where so many, otherwise good
players, break down altogether. They
seem to be unable to realise the most

important fact that an opponent's hand
consists of only thirteen cards. I have
seen a player sacrifice his whole hand in
order to keep a double guard to a queen,
when he knew, or would have known if
he had taken the trouble to count, that
it was an absolute impossibility that his
opponent could have more than two of
that suit. Quite the most common form
of giving away a game at No Trumps is
by a player thinking it necessary to keep
a double guard to a queen, and throwing
away winning cards in order to do so,
when the game was irretrievably lost,
unless his partner held either the ace or
king. This is of everyday occurrence,
and the reason of it is that players will
not, or cannot, count the dealer's hand.
If it is possible for the dealer to hold
ace, king, and another of that suit, and

the making of the queen will save the
game, then keep the double guard by
all means, but when that one trick will
not save the game, throw away one, or
both guards, and trust to your partner
holding the ace or king. One extra
trick lost, even if it entail the loss of the
small slam, is no great matter; but a
game lost, when it could otherwise have
been saved, is a very serious and expensive calamity.

It is nothing but a waste of time to
attempt the impossible. If the dealer,
in his own hand and dummy's combined,
has strength in all four suits, the game is
lost, and there is no help for it, and all
that can be done is to save as much as
possible; but very few No Trump hands
are of the cast-iron order; there is nearly
always a vulnerable spot somewhere, and

the one aim and object of the first-class bridge-player is to locate that vulnerable spot as soon as he can by drawing any inferences that his ingenuity can suggest to him. He is always on the look-out for these inferences, and they appear very obvious to his trained understanding, while they remain as a sealed book to the less observant and less experienced player. The object of this little treatise is to endeavour to break that seal, and open the book to any one who cares to investigate the contents of it, even though at first he may get but a passing glimpse.

CHAPTER III

THE best and most valuable inferences
that can be drawn from the declaration
are invariably negative ones, that is to
say, it is not nearly so much from what
the dealer declares as from what he does
not declare that such inferences are to
be drawn. He cannot possibly avoid
giving away information in this manner.
When he declares an attacking suit, such
as hearts or diamonds, it does not require
the wisdom of Solomon to infer that he
holds pronounced strength in the suit
declared, but the matter does not end

with that—there is a reverse side to the
medal. When the dealer, at the score
of love, passes the declaration, he an-
nounces, to everybody who will listen
and take heed, that he does not hold, in
his own hand, either the nucleus of a No
Trump call or sufficient strength to declare either hearts or diamonds. He may
have protection in one or both of those
suits, but he certainly has not got attacking strength in either.

The more advanced the state of the
dealer's score, the more strongly does this
inference apply. If he passes the declaration with his score at 18, he can see
no reasonable possibility of winning two
by cards on a diamond declaration. A
somewhat light diamond call, which
would be a very bad one at the score of
love, becomes a good one with the dealer's

score at 18 or over.   If he leaves it to his
partner when he is already 24 up, he
gives you still more information.   Not
only does he tell you that he has not got
an attacking hand on any valuable declaration, but also that he cannot see his
way to two by cards in clubs, or to three
in spades, with the assistance of an
average hand from his partner.   He may
possibly be a little bit hampered by the
fear of being doubled if he makes at all a
doubtful declaration, but you may depend
upon it that if a sound player can see a
fair chance of winning the game on any
declaration, red or black, he will have a
go for it, regardless of consequences.

It is a very useful practice to ask
yourself, at an advanced point in the
dealer's score, what declaration he ought
to make, or is likely to make, or what

declaration you would wish to make
yourself if you were in his place, and could
see a reasonable chance of winning the
game on that hand. If he does not make
that obvious declaration, or one of those
obvious declarations, you may be quite
sure that the reason for his not doing so
is that the requisite materials are lacking
to him. At the score of 22, the obvious
declaration would be hearts or clubs. At
24, it would be either hearts or diamonds,
with diamonds for choice, as there would
be an equal chance of winning the game,
with less danger if things went wrong.
At 26 the club declaration stands out
strongly, as the odd trick will win the
game, and even a double will not be very
expensive. At 26 or 28 an attacking
spade declaration enters into the field of
calculation, and a good player will never

hesitate to declare spades originally, when
he can see a good chance of winning the
game on that declaration, quite regardless
of larger chances which he may forgo
by so doing. When the dealer does not
do any of these obvious things, there is
the inference—patent to the most unobservant—that he does not possess the
requisite strength.

These are the principal inferences to
be drawn from the ordinary declarations
by the dealer. From the declaration
by the dummy there are none, as the
necessary exposure of the hand at once
discloses the whole situation. There re-
mains the original black-suit declaration.
In these enlightened days this is, happily,
of rare occurrence, especially among good
players ; but there are players of a
timorous nature who persist in declaring

spades as dealer when they have a bad hand, as a purely protective measure, and therefore the point must be considered.

When an original spade declaration is made by the dealer, you are perfectly safe in inferring that he has an absolutely impotent hand. He may possibly have a considerable number of spades—such as six or seven headed by the knave or queen ; but, outside the spade suit, it is an absolute certainty that he has nothing at all. It is rather a dangerous time to double on outside cards, without strength in the spade suit, but it is a very easy hand to play against. You can lead strengthening cards up to the dealer, and the third player can finesse against him to any extent, knowing for certain that he has nothing of value in his hand at all. The original spade declaration is called a "defensive" measure, but it certainly puts very offensive weapons into the hands of its opponents.

An original club declaration is quite another matter. The days of defensive club declarations are past and gone. No sane person would nowadays make an original club declaration because he had a bad hand, but the club declaration is occasionally made, by good players, when they have a practical certainty of the odd trick or more, with a good honour score, and they elect to take that small certainty in preference to speculating on larger but doubtful possibilities by passing to their partner. The original club declaration should only be read as great strength in the club suit, and no other card of entry. Make a special note of that—no other

3

card of entry—otherwise the dealer would
not have declared clubs, he would have
declared No Trumps if his club suit were
established; if not, he would have left it
to his partner.   There is your inference
standing out, clear and well defined.   The
dealer has great strength in clubs, but he
is practically powerless in the other three
suits.

Having finished with inferences to be
drawn from the declaration, I can imagine
some of our bridge-playing readers saying:
"This may be all very nice and very
true, but we knew it all before.   Tell us
something that we do not know."   To
such I would answer: "Of course you
know it.   These things are self-evident
to any one who will take the trouble to
think about the matter at all; but do
you apply them?   Do you draw these

inferences in actual play at the card table; do you make a mental note of them at the time; do you remember them, and do you act on them? When the dealer passes the declaration, whatever may be the state of the score, does it convey anything to you; do you try to realise, not what he has got in his hand, but what he has not got, what he cannot have; and do you endeavour to frame your game upon the information thus acquired?"

It is no earthly use being able to draw inferences if you do not apply them and act on them. Directly the dummy hand is exposed, the knowledge of what the dealer has not got will help you enormously to guess what your partner has got, and this is the principal means by which that much-talked-of counting of the

cards is brought about. Take just one
instance. Suppose the dealer has not
declared hearts, and neither you nor the
dummy hold an honour in hearts, is it
not an absolute certainty that your
partner must have at least two or three
honours and probably more, as the dealer
would certainly have declared hearts with
64 in his hand ?

By extending the same principle a
little further you can sometimes place a
long suit of hearts in your partner's
hand. Let us suppose that the dealer,
who is already 16 up, passes the declaration. You have only two hearts in your
own hand, and dummy puts down only
two. Now, who has got those hearts ?
They are not under the table—somebody
has got to hold them, and the dealer
cannot be strong in them or he would

have declared hearts to the score, therefore the majority of them must be in your partner's hand. Such inferences as these present themselves in almost every hand to any one who will look out for them and heed them. .

When the dealer has made an original declaration of No Trumps, the inference that he has a high card, presumably the ace or king, in at least three suits, is surely very obvious, and yet many players quite fail to recognise it even in the first lead of the game. The sort of case which constantly occurs is as follows: The original leader opens with the 7 of a suit, the dummy puts down knave, 6, 4, and the third player holds queen, 8, 3. A very easy application of the Eleven Rule shows the third player that the dealer has one card, and one only, higher than the 7, and that one card may be either the ace, king, 10, or 9. The third player cannot possibly tell which one of those four cards the dealer holds, but surely he can infer something about it. The dealer having declared the No Trump, is extremely likely to hold either the ace or king, in fact, he is almost marked with one of them, especially if high cards in other suits are to be seen in the dummy, therefore the third player, acting on his inference that the dealer must hold either ace or king, should pass the 7 led, and, if his inference be right, the whole suit is at once established. There is, of course, the possibility that his partner may have led from ace, king, in which case a valuable trick, and probably the game as well, has been given away; but for every once that this inference

proves to be wrong it will be right ten
times, and nothing is more irritating than
to see one's partner pop on the queen
in such a case, without thinking for a
moment about the probable placing of
the other cards—he will then tell you
that he believes in the old maxim, " third
hand plays high." That maxim, good
as it was at Whist, is responsible for a
great deal of damage in the No Trump
game at Bridge.

CHAPTER IV

WE now come to inferences to be drawn from the way in which the dealer elects to play his cards after the dummy hand is exposed. Here again, and still more strongly, it is not so much from what he does as from what he does not do that valuable inferences may often be drawn.

In a No Trump game, when there is a long, unestablished suit of five or six cards in dummy, and the dealer does not at once go for that suit, it becomes a certainty that he has not got the requisite cards to establish it and to bring it in.

The most common form in which this
presents itself is when the dummy puts
down five or more cards of a suit headed
by queen, knave, or possibly even by
queen, knave, 10. If the dealer, directly
he gets in, does not go for this suit, the
inference should be obvious to the meanest
understanding—he has neither the ace
nor the king in his own hand, as in both
cases the suit could be established at
once, therefore either of the opponents
who holds one of the two high cards can
safely place the other one in his partner's
hand. Quite recently I lost a big rubber
which we could easily have won, entirely
through my partner failing to draw this
particular inference when it was very
obvious.

The score was one game all and eighteen
to twelve against us. The dealer left it,

and dummy declared No Trumps on the following hand:

> Hearts—Ace, queen
> Diamonds—Queen, 10, 5
> Clubs—Ace, 10, 4
> Spades—Queen, knave, 9, 6, 2

It was my lead, and I led the knave of hearts. The first five tricks were:

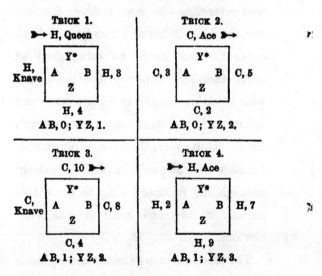

TRICK 1.

➤ H, Queen

H, Knave   A   Y*   B   H, 3
               Z
           H, 4
AB, 0; YZ, 1.

TRICK 2.

C, Ace ➤

C, 3   A   Y*   B   C, 5
           Z
       C, 2
AB, 0; YZ, 2.

TRICK 3.

C, 10 ➤

C, Knave   A   Y*   B   C, 8
               Z
           C, 4
AB, 1; YZ, 2.

TRICK 4.

➤ H, Ace

H, 2   A   Y*   B   H, 7
           Z
       H, 9
AB, 1; YZ, 3.

* Dummy.

TRICK 5.

C, 4

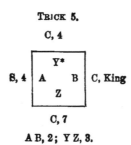

8, 4   A   B   C, King

C, 7

A B, 2; Y Z, 3.

My partner then had to lead. His hand
originally was :

Hearts—9, 3
Diamonds—King, 9, 7, 6, 3
Clubs—King, 8, 5
Spades—King, 10, 3

He was left with his five diamonds and
three spades, and the question was how
to put me in to make the winning hearts,
which were clearly marked in my hand.
After studying the position carefully, he
led a small diamond. The dealer, who

* Dummy.

held the ace, passed it up; the queen
won, and he then put himself in with
the ace of diamonds, made his two long
clubs, and won the game. Having lost
the game and rubber, my partner said
that it was very unlucky, but that he
thought the best chance of putting me in
was that I should have the ace of diamonds, especially as I had discarded a
spade. It happened that I had only one
diamond, the knave, which would have
been a very bad discard; and, apart
from any question of the discard, was it
conceivable that the dealer could have
had that ace of spades ? He, the dealer,
was a very good player, and if he had
held the ace of spades he would have had
a certainty of winning the odd trick by
attacking at once in the spade suit; but
he had not done so. He had carefully

kept off that suit—as a matter of fact
he had only the 5—and the ace of spades
was as plainly marked in my hand, to
any one with an ordinary power of drawing
deductions, as if it had been exposed on
the table. After the third trick I had
marked the king of spades in my partner's
hand, and he ought, with equal certainty,
to have marked the ace in my hand.
You must credit your opponent with
some modicum of ordinary intelligence,
and when he does not adopt the obvious
course to win the game, it is quite safe
to conclude that he has not got the
requisite card or cards. This is just
ordinary deduction. It may sometimes
be wrong. The dealer may occasionally
lay a trap for you, but depend upon it
that, if he can see a chance of winning
the game by plain, straightforward

methods, he will do so, and when he does not adopt those plain methods, it is because he has not got the wherewithal.

When the dealer does not go for a long suit which you see exposed in his dummy, it is either because he has a better suit in his own hand, or because he cannot see his way to establish and bring in dummy's suit. In nine cases out of ten the dealer in a No Trump game will attack at once in the suit of which he has the greatest number in his two hands combined. If you are very weak in one suit, say you have only one or two small ones, and the dealer does not attack in that suit, you can with safety credit your partner with strength in it, and you can sometimes help him very much by leading it for him. The following hand was

a striking instance of this : No Trumps
was declared by the dummy, who put
down :

>Hearts—Ace, 9, 3
>Diamonds—King, 10, 4
>Clubs—King, queen, 7, 2
>Spades—King, knave, 4

The eldest hand led the 5 of hearts,
holding

>Hearts—King, knave, 7, 5, 4, 2
>Diamonds—8, 7, 4
>Clubs—Ace, 8, 3
>Spades—7

His partner played the 10 of hearts,
which the dealer won with the queen.
The dealer then led the knave of clubs,
and the eldest hand won it with his ace.
Now, surely, the dealer's play ought to
have conveyed some useful information
to an intelligent adversary. There were
nine spades divided between the third

player and the dealer, and the king, knave, and another were on the table. If the dealer had five spades with an honour of any kind, would he not have gone for that suit at once? But he had not done so, and therefore the third player was marked with at least five spades, and a lead through the king, knave must have been an advantage to him—as a matter of fact he had six headed by ace, queen, and the ace of diamonds to bring them in with. Do you think that he got that lead of a spade which he was praying for? Not a chance. The eldest hand went solidly on with his own suit of hearts, and the result was that he and his partner made nothing but their three aces and the queen of spades, losing three by cards, instead of winning the odd trick, as they must have done if the

eldest hand had had the faculty of drawing an ordinary plain inference. His
excuse was that he hoped his partner
might have two hearts left, so that he
would be able to bring in all the long
hearts, but here was another inference
missed. There were only two hearts
not accounted for, the 8 and another,
and his partner could not have the
8, as he had played the 10 on the
first round with the 9 exposed in
dummy, therefore he could not have
more than one heart left. Here you
see that even a comparatively un-
important card such as a 10 instead
of an 8 may have an important sig-
nification—in fact, almost every card
that is played conveys its message to
the player who has the faculty of
reading it correctly, and successful

4

bridge is largely governed by and based upon these messages, and upon the inferences which skilful players draw from them.

CHAPTER V

A VERY good instance of the sort of inference that can be drawn from what the dealer does not do is the following, quoted from an Illustrative Hand in "Bridge Abridged." The dealer, Z, at the score of love all, passed the declaration. The dummy declared No Trumps, and put down :

Hearts—Ace, queen
Diamonds—King, 9, 3
Clubs—Ace, queen, 10, 5, 4
Spades—Ace, king, 6

The first three tricks were :

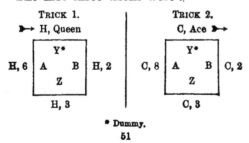

TRICK 1.

TRICK 2.

* Dummy.

TRICK 3.

C, 4 ▶→

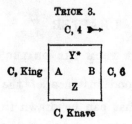

C, King

C, 6

C, Knave

Now, what inferences could be drawn
from the way in which the dealer en-
gineered this hand, or rather from the
way in which he did not engineer it?
Just study the dummy hand—a very
strong one—for a moment, and ask
yourself how you would have elected to
go on with the game if you had been
in the dealer's place, after winning the
first trick with the queen of hearts. Does
not the dealer's play at tricks 2 and 3
convey any information to you? If he
had any card of entry in his own hand,

* Dummy.

would he not have put himself in at once
and have led the knave of clubs up to
the ace, queen, 10 in dummy, so as to
ensure every trick in that suit, if the
king happened to lie right for him, with
the certainty of winning the game, whether
the finesse was successful or not ? Instead of doing this. he purposely gave
away one trick in the club suit, and
thereby confessed his weakness. He
could at once be marked with no card
of entry in his own hand, and therefore
the queen of spades and the ace and queen
of diamonds were all against him, and
either of his opponents, who did not hold
any of these three cards, ought at once
to have placed them in his partner's
hand. Think what an advantage knowledge of this kind may give towards the
end of a hand, to know for certain that

your partner has a winning card or cards
in a particular suit. You can put him
in whenever you want to, or you can so
arrange the game as to get him led up
to, and you can discard from that suit
with the greatest confidence, knowing
that he can protect it; and yet a
large number of regular bridge players
habitually miss these golden oppor-
tunities, the reason being that they
fail to notice these inferences at the
moment when the opportunity occurs.
It is no earthly use trying to think back
and to draw inferences from what occurred three or four tricks ago. These
inferences must be drawn at the time and
made a mental note of and remembered
—that is the only way in which they will
be of real practical use.

In a No Trump game, when the dealer

holds up a winning card, generally the ace, of the suit originally opened, until the last possible moment, this proceeding should give great encouragement to the opponents. It shows that the game is not a certainty. The dealer is afraid of the establishment of that suit, and there are certainly one or two winning cards of other suits out against him. On the other hand, when he is in a hurry to win the first trick, as for instance by putting on the queen from ace, queen, and another in dummy, instead of letting it come up to his own hand, it generally signifies that there is another suit of which he is more afraid, so he tries to prevent the third hand winning the first trick for fear that he will branch into the other suit.

It may be regarded as certain that the

dealer will go straight for the game, without taking any risks, as soon as he can see a certainty, or even a strong probability, of winning it; therefore, when you find that he is playing a weak game, by taking deep finesses, or possibly by putting you in with your own suit so as to make you open another suit up to him, you should harden your heart and play boldly for a better result than the bare saving of the game.

Most No Trump hands are either very good or very bad. Either the dummy hand nicks in well with the dealer's, or it is of very little use to him. If it nicks in well success is practically assured, but if it does not nick in well it sometimes becomes a rather dangerous asset. If the dummy puts down five cards of a suit in which the dealer is very weak, it un-

doubtedly affords him a certain amount
of protection, but it may also afford the
adversaries very useful information.   If
the dealer carefully avoids that suit, and
perhaps discards from it, the missing high
cards in it are plainly marked against him,
and, towards the close of the hand, it
may be of supreme importance for one
of his adversaries to know how he can
put his partner in.   Suppose that the
dummy has the queen and four small
clubs, if the dealer does not touch that
suit it is quite certain that he has not got
both the ace and king, and very probable
that he has neither of them.   If the
dummy holds queen, knave, 10, or queen,
knave, 9 of a suit of which you have the
king, and the dealer does not lead the
queen when he gets into dummy's hand,
you can safely conclude that he has not

got the ace himself. These inferences could be multiplied indefinitely. The way to make use of them is to ask yourself how the dealer would be likely to play the hand if he held certain named cards, and, when he does not play as you imagine he would do if he had them, to make up your mind at once that he has not got those named cards.

There is one notable ruse which is worth mentioning, as it is occasionally made use of by good players. When the dealer, in a No Trump game, is absolutely undefended in one suit, both in his own hand and in his dummy, and he is fortunate enough not to have had that suit opened, he will sometimes lead the highest card of it at once from dummy, directly he gets in, with the object of stalling his opponents off it by inducing them to

believe that he has great strength in it
himself. You should be careful not to
be deceived by this artifice. It is nothing
but a bluff, and rather a desperate bluff,
but I have known it to be brought off
with great success on more than one occasion. Weak players are very easily put
off by this manœuvre, but the strong
player will generally see through it, and,
as soon as the dummy hand gets the lead
again the situation is bound to be dis-
closed, as he cannot afford to do it a
second time.

It is very much easier for the dealer
to draw correct inferences, and to read
his opponents' hands, than for them to
read his, for the simple reason that he
knows that they will not play false cards.
When one of the defenders in a No Trump
game plays a king, the dealer can at once

place the queen in the other player's
hand, if he has not got it himself; but as
regards the dealer's play this is not so,
rather the reverse.

The habit of playing false cards as
dealer has become so ingrained into the
minds of most players that an intelligent
adversary can often draw quite correct
inferences by interpreting the dealer's
play upside down, so to speak. For instance, when the dealer wins a trick with
a king, there is no ground whatever for
inferring that he has not got the queen;
but the great majority of players play
false cards as dealer so systematically,
on every possible occasion, that, when
one of them plays a queen, it is quite a
logical conclusion to infer that he has not
got the king, or he would have played it
in preference to the queen.

Some few players purposely vary their
tactics, so as not to give away information; but they are the exception, not the
rule. The ordinary player has very little
variety. The methods which he adopts
on one occasion he is almost certain to
reproduce on another, and I have scored
many a point, and saved many a game,
by drawing what I call the reverse inference, that when the dealer plays a
high card he has not got a higher one of
equal value, or he would have been
certain to false-card. This little tip is
well worth remembering, and you will
find that the inference will work out
correctly time after time.

Correct inference is nothing more than
the card sense highly developed. To
some players, some few players, it comes
naturally, to others it comes as the result

of much practice and of close observation;
but it is quite open to anybody who will
take the trouble to cultivate it assiduously,
who will watch the fall of the cards carefully, and draw deductions at the time.

CHAPTER VI

INFERENCE FROM THE DISCARD

THE dealer's discards, both from his own hand and from dummy, will often give you valuable information, although you must bear in mind that he will try to deceive you as much as possible. You may always be quite sure that he will not throw away any cards which are likely to become winners later in the hand unless he is absolutely obliged to do so in order to protect another suit. When he has to make one or two discards early in the hand, those discards will certainly not be from his strong suit, nor will they be from a suit in which he is very weak; they will nearly always be from a suit in which he is protected, either in his own hand or in dummy, such as ace and two small ones, or king and three small ones.

When he discards, from his own hand, a suit in which dummy is strong, or well protected, it tells you nothing. It is obviously not necessary for him to keep strength, or even protection, in both hands; but when he discards from a suit in which dummy is very weak it does tell you something. It tells you that that is not his own long suit, or that, if it is his best suit, the rest of his hand must be very bad. He may be, and probably is, protected in that suit, but he can have no attacking strength in it, and it at once becomes a good suit to lead through him up to the dummy's weakness.

If the dealer discards one or two small cards from a long unestablished suit in dummy, it shows plainly that he has no hope of establishing and bringing in that suit. If he discards from an established suit in dummy in preference to unguarding a high card in another suit, he is either very weak himself in the other suit or he requires that high card in order to bring in the established suit. If he discards from a four-card suit in dummy he has probably got four of the same suit in his own hand, and he does not require all dummy's four cards. If he retains two small and worthless cards in dummy which he could well have discarded, it should show you that he wants to lead that suit twice up to his own hand for purposes of finessing.

The dealer will deceive you by any

5

means in his power, but he will not give away tricks in order to deceive you, and he cannot avoid occasionally giving you very useful information by his discards.

Here again—the same thing keeps cropping up—it will be more by what he does not discard than by what he does discard. That is the real crux of the whole business—to try to ascribe a reason for everything that he does when it is at all different from what you expect him to do.

With a declared trump suit there are not so many inferences to be drawn from the dealer's play, but there are some.

The most important is when he does not take the trumps out at once. The ordinary procedure, with a strong trump declaration, is for the dealer to lead

trumps directly he gets in. If he does
not follow the usual practice he must have
a reason for not doing so. Either he
wants to make a ruff in the weak hand,
or he is playing to establish a long suit,
or his trumps are not strong enough to
get all the others out.

It must be one of these three situations,
and you should try to defeat his object,
whatever it may be. In nine cases out
of ten, if the dealer does not lead trumps,
his opponents ought to lead them for
him. If he does not want the trumps
out, it follows that his opponents do. If
he is trying for a ruff in the weak hand,
his opponents should lead trumps without
hesitation, even at the cost of leading
up to the declaring hand. If he is trying
to establish a long suit in the weak hand,
the best policy is to make winning cards

as quickly as possible before the declaring
hand can get any discards.

When the strength is in dummy, and
the dealer wishes to get the lead into his
own hand, the way in which he attempts
to do so may be very instructive to an
observant adversary. It is obvious that,
if he holds an ace, or a high trump, he
can put himself in at once, and he will
proceed to do so; but if, instead of doing
this, he tries to get in with a guarded
king or queen, there is a strong inference
that he has not got a certain card of entry,
and consequently any missing high cards
can at once be marked by either adversary
as being in his partner's hand. When
the dealer does not lead from a queen,
knave suit in dummy, both the ace and
king are probably against him. When
he leads a small card up to an ace, knave,

ten suit in dummy, it becomes quite
certain that he has not got the queen
himself. When there is only one trump,
the best one, in against him, and he leads
a losing trump to get rid of it, you may
be quite sure that he has got, in one
hand or the other, an established suit
which he can bring in, and you should
make any winning cards that you are
fortunate enough to have as quickly as
possible, before he has time to get discards.

When an attacking suit declaration
has been made by the dealer, the result
of the game will generally depend upon
the strength or weakness of the dummy
hand in the other suits. Even if the
dummy puts down four or five trumps
there is nothing to be frightened about,
unless he has strength in other suits as

well. What the dealer probably wanted
to find was "side cards," that is, aces
and kings of other suits. You may be
quite sure that the dealer has not got a
lot of winning cards outside his trumps,
or he would have declared No Trumps,
and if the dummy is short of aces and
kings in other suits, the game is almost
certain to be saved, however many trumps
there may be in the two hands.

When a spade declaration has been
doubled, the complexion of the game is
altered altogether. The defenders now
become the attacking party, and should
play their hands for all they are worth.
The dealer, by passing the declaration,
has confessed to having, at best, only a
moderate hand, and, if he produces fairly
good cards in one or two suits, it is quite
safe to infer that he is very weak in the

other two. That confession of weakness
by the dealer should never be lost sight
of. The exact measure of his weakness
must remain an uncertainty. He may
be very weak indeed, or he may be just
short of a No Trump call—time will show ;
anyhow, he has told you that he has not
sufficient strength to declare No Trumps,
or either red suit, and that information
is bound to give you some very useful
data to work upon.

In any case, whether it is a No Trump
or a suit declaration, the first thing which
the good bridge player invariably does
is to put himself in the dealer's place,
and to determine in his own mind how
he would proceed to play the hand,
gauging the dealer's hand by the minimum
strength which he ought to have to justify
the declaration which he has made. If

the declaration happens to be a very
strong one, and the dummy puts down
a fairly helping hand, the game is lost,
and there is no help for it; but this is the
exception, not the rule.   On most hands,
with most declarations, there is a weak
spot somewhere, and the first-rate player
is always looking for that weak spot, and
is always trying to draw inferences from
the dealer's play which may lead him to
it.   These inferences are by no means
certainties when they are arrived at, they
are only probabilities; but is it not
much better to have even probabilities
to work upon than to go on groping about
in the dark, knowing no more about the
hand than the cards that have been
actually played, and drawing no deductions, correct or incorrect, however
unusual the dealer's method of engineer-

ing his two hands may have been ? I
much prefer a partner who draws wrong
inferences to one who does not draw any
at all. There is some hope for the former,
but none for the latter. The faculty of
drawing correct inferences is one which
develops very quickly with practice, and,
even if you are sometimes wrong at first,
every inference drawn, whether right or
wrong, will make the next one easier,
until you will be quite surprised to find
how much information the game contains,
and how easy it is to read between the
lines.

Deductions, or inferences, are the whole
life and soul of first-class scientific bridge,
and when the expert player brings off
some remarkable coup, which is perhaps
talked about and quoted as an instance
of skilful play, he is nearly always acting

on " information received," as they say
at Scotland Yard, and this information
is not, as in the case of the Scotland Yard
authorities, vouchsafed to his private
ear alone, but is tendered openly at the
bridge table for the benefit of anybody
who has the power to apply it and to
make use of it.

CHAPTER VII

COUNTING THE HANDS

IN the preceding chapters of this treatise
I have endeavoured to point out the most
obvious ways in which inferences can be
drawn, and how certain high cards can
sometimes be marked in one's partner's
hand by inferring that it is not possible,
or at any rate extremely unlikely, that
the adversary can hold them. This will
often prove of great assistance in the
successful play of a hand, but inferences
have another, and a still more important,
use in helping one to count the cards
towards the end of the deal.

Counting the cards correctly, when
there are three or four left in each hand,

may well be described as the highest
possible flight of scientific bridge. It
has been much talked about, and much
written about, and some writers on the
game seem to imagine that every one
who plays bridge possesses the faculty
of doing it, but this is by no means the
case. All first-class players try for it,
and do it, with more or less success, but
to the great bulk of players it is an altogether unexploited field of enterprise,
and yet it is so easy if inferences have
been drawn at the proper time and remembered. The process must begin from
the very commencement of the hand—
from the first lead. Against a No Trump
declaration, if the leader begins with a 2,
he is then and there marked with exactly
four cards of that suit, and with no five-
card suit in his hand. If he begins with

a card that is not necessarily his lowest,
he has at least four of the suit, and very
likely more. The second round will
probably enable you to gauge the exact
number of his holding, and directly you
have acquired that knowledge you should
make a mental note of it and remember
it—you will then have a certain number
of cards in his hand accounted for, and
this can hardly fail to make it easier to
count the rest of his hand. It is obvious
that when a player has a great number
of one suit in his hand, he is bound to be
comparatively short in the other suits.
An average hand contains three of each
suit, with one odd card somewhere.
Directly a hand is found to have considerably more or less than the average
number in one suit, there is bound to be
a proportionate decrease or increase in

the other suits. Quite the best instance of counting a whole hand from the original lead that I ever came across was given as a problem in a contemporary last summer.

No Trumps were declared by the dummy. The dummy's hand and the third player's were :

Hearts—Ace, 7, 4
Diamonds—Ace, 9, 3
Clubs—King, queen, 9, 5, 3
Spades—Ace, 6

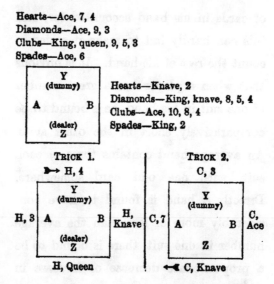

The play of the first two tricks was given as above, and the question asked was : " What ought B to lead at trick 3, and why ? " The solution of the problem turned entirely on A's original lead having been from a four-card suit, and on the inference to be drawn therefrom that he could not have more than four of another suit. Directly he played the 7 of clubs at trick 2 his partner B could be certain that he had no more clubs, and could therefore count his whole hand—four hearts, four diamonds, four spades, and one club. Being primed with this know-ledge, B could account for twelve dia-monds, leaving Z, the dealer, with only one, which might possibly be the queen, therefore B must lead the king of dia-monds instead of returning his partner's heart, as he would then be certain to

win four tricks in the diamond suit.
That was the answer to the problem, and
I believe I am correct in stating that
every one of the solvers answered it
correctly; but I wonder how many of
them would have realised the position
in actual play at the bridge table. The
hand was said to have occurred in actual
play, but we were not told whether it
was played correctly; however, by a
curious coincidence, almost identically
the same hand occurred about the same
time in a bridge tournament in America,
and in that case it was played correctly.

It is very rarely indeed that a whole
hand can be counted in this way. It is
generally in the last four or five cards
that the counting takes place. Have
you never noticed a good bridge player
hesitate for a moment or two towards

the end of a hand and appear to think the position out carefully ? He is not thinking what to play next ; he is endeavouring to place the remaining cards in the other hands. He perhaps knows, from deductions drawn earlier, that the player on his left holds two clubs, no hearts, and no spades—his remaining two cards must be diamonds. Ridiculously easy, is it not ? and yet, easy as it seems, many players never attempt the process of counting in this way at all. I remember once hearing a player ask, in an aggrieved tone, " How could I possibly tell that So-and-so had three diamonds ? " when there were three cards left in each hand, and all the other three suits had been exhausted, and not a card except diamonds was left at all.

The successful counting of the hands

is nearly always arrived at by a sort of process of elimination. The knowledge of what an opponent has not got will help enormously in estimating what he has got; thus, if he has played void in hearts and diamonds, it is very plain that his remaining cards must be clubs and spades, and the only doubtful point is how many of each he holds.

It is much easier for the dealer to count his opponents' hands than for them to count his, because he knows that they will not play false cards for fear of deceiving one another, whereas he, having no partner to deceive, can play his cards just as he likes. This counting must begin from the very first lead, although it may not be brought into use until the end of the hand. It is in placing the lead during the last three or four tricks that

it comes in so useful, and that the result
of a game will sometimes depend upon it.

Let us take a very simple little instance
—hearts are trumps. The dealer, requiring
two more tricks to win the game, is left
with queen and 7 of hearts and ace and
queen of spades. He knows that his
left-hand adversary has the king and 10
of trumps, no diamonds and no clubs,
therefore he must have two spades.
The dealer leads a trump, right up to
the tenace over him; but the adversary
is then obliged to lead a spade, and the
required two tricks are assured.

The exact value of the cards held does
not matter so much as the number of
each suit. When there are only four
cards left in each hand, it may be of untold
value for the dealer to be able to say to
himself, " A has two diamonds and two

clubs, and B has one diamond, two spades, and one club," and it really is not so very difficult to arrive at some conclusion of the kind if the previous fall of the cards has been carefully watched and correct inferences drawn. Of course, it cannot always, or even often, be done so completely as that, but towards the end of every hand the dealer ought to be able to place some of the cards in each of his opponent's hands, and to make a pretty shrewd guess as to the others.

His opponents' discards will help him very considerably. Suppose that the dummy has king, knave, and another of a suit which has not been led, if the player on the dealer's left discards one or two cards of that suit it at once becomes patent that he has not got the queen. He may have the ace, in fact, he probably

has got it, but he would never have discarded his guards to the queen with the
king, knave lying over him. Again, the
convention of the discard from weakness, which is almost universal in English
bridge, is a great aid to the dealer in
placing missing high cards. Not only
should he watch the discards very carefully, and make a mental note of what
suit each of his opponents shows weakness
in, but sometimes, when he is left with
the last two trumps in a suit declaration,
it will pay him to lead out the trumps, in
order to force discards from his opponents,
and to find out on which side to take
a finesse. Much useful information can
occasionally be gleaned in this way.

Every one who aspires to become a
good bridge player should make a point
of trying to place the cards towards the

end of every hand. Let him try to place one or two at first, and see how near he can get to a correct diagnosis. This faculty of placing cards is one which will be found to improve to quite a surprising extent with constant practice. When he has succeeded in placing one or two correctly, let him essay a still higher flight ; and when he one day succeeds, as he will do, in placing every card correctly, he can flatter himself that he is within measurable distance of being a really first-class bridge player.

Printed in the USA
CPSIA information can be obtained
at www.ICGtesting.com
LVHW011410101223
766115LV00015B/1330